DRAGONS

monster
Chronicles

Monster
Chronicles

Dragons

Stephen Krensky

Lerner Publications Company · Minneapolis

Lerner Publications Company
A division of Lerner Publishing Group
241 First Avenue North
Minneapolis, MN 55401 U.S.A.

Website address: www.lernerbooks.com

Library of Congress Cataloging-in-Publication Data

Krensky, Stephen.
    Dragons / by Stephen Krensky.
        p.   cm. — (Monster chronicles)
    Includes bibliographical references and index.
    ISBN-13: 978-0-8225-6543-7 (lib. bdg. : alk. paper)
    ISBN-10: 0-8225-6543-9 (lib. bdg. : alk. paper)
    1. Dragons—Juvenile literature. I. Title. II. Series.
    GR830.D7K74 2007
    398'.469—dc22   2006010833

Manufactured in the United States of America
1 2 3 4 5 6 - JR - 12 11 10 09 08 07

TABLE OF CONTENTS

1 WORLD-FAMOUS MONSTERS

Dragons may be the most popular monsters ever created. But being popular doesn't make them the most likable monsters. It doesn't make them the friendliest either. It just makes them the monsters that show up in the most

places. Dragons are famous all over the world—from Asia to the Middle East, from Europe to the Americas.

According to tales and legends, dragons don't live in cities or any other places with lots of people. They live deep underground or high up on mountaintops. They swim in the sea or fly through the air. Many dragons breathe fire. Some dragons perform magic. Others know how to talk. Some dragons are big, and others are small. But no matter what they look like, dragons are hard to ignore.

DRAGONS IN ANCIENT TIMES

People have believed in dragons for a long time. As long as people have been writing down history—more than five thousand years—they have told stories about dragons. People's pictures of dragons are even older.

Dragons started out as powerful beings, and they stayed that way. They flew through the air, breathed fire, and weren't afraid to throw their weight around. Dragons were rarely shy. They didn't mind their own business. They came and went as they pleased.

The earliest dragons appear in writings from the Middle East and Asia. In the Middle East, the ancient Egyptians, Sumerians, Babylonians, and Assyrians all believed in dragons. In these cultures, dragons looked like giant snakes. Few of them were friendly.

Some early dragons, such as the one pictured below, looked like giant snakes with small wings.

Thousands of miles away, Asian dragons had much better public relations. In ancient China, the dragon was a symbol of great power. The throne where the Chinese emperor sat was called the dragon throne. According to Chinese folklore, Chinese emperors were descended from dragons.

Images of the dragon decorated the Chinese emperor's home, the Imperial Palace in Beijing (*above*). The emperor's throne was called the dragon seat, and his bed was called the dragon bed.

The Chinese believed in many kinds of dragons. Some Chinese dragons guarded treasures. Other Chinese dragons ruled water, such as rain and rivers. When there was too much water (a flood) or too little water (a drought), Chinese villagers held religious services. During the services, people asked local dragons for help. The villagers hoped the dragons would either bring more water or take extra water away.

YEAR OF THE DRAGON

According to one Chinese legend, the Buddha—the founder of the Buddhist religion—told all the animals on Earth to come to him. In the end, only twelve animals completed the journey. These animals were the dragon, rat, ox, tiger, rabbit, snake, horse, sheep, monkey, rooster, dog, and boar. They became the symbols of the Chinese zodiac *(above)*.

Each animal in the Chinese zodiac stands for a certain year. That animal influences the traits of people born during the year. For instance, someone born in the Year of the Dragon will be confident, fearless, and proud.

The next Year of the Dragon will be 2012.

People in ancient Japan also respected dragons. They too believed that their emperor was descended from dragons. In fact, both the Japanese and the Chinese claimed the first dragons on earth as their own. In each place, people viewed dragons from the other country as inferior to their own magnificent creatures.

Dragons Head West

The rise of European civilization led to an increase in dragon sightings. The famous Greek thinker Aristotle wrote about dragons, which he called flying serpents. In a book called *The History of Animals* (350 B.C.), Aristotle explained that dragons lived in Ethiopia, in Africa. According to him, dragons were no more unusual than any other animal.

According to Greek myth, the goddess Demeter traveled in a chariot pulled by two dragons.

The Roman writer Pliny the Elder described dragons in his book *Natural History* (A.D. 77). Like Aristotle, he noted that dragons lived in Ethiopia. Ethiopian dragons, Pliny said, were not as big as the dragons of India. But they were still quite big—about sixty feet long. In addition to dragons, Pliny's book included other imaginary creatures, including unicorns, as well as real animals such as elephants. Neither Aristotle nor Pliny ever saw any dragons themselves. They simply heard stories about dragons and included them in their books.

People in ancient Europe thought that dragons were ordinary animals—although big and powerful ones. The earliest European dragons didn't speak or perform magic. No one in ancient Europe thought of dragons as evil.

But when Christianity began to spread through Europe two thousand years ago, Christian leaders took a good look around. They decided that fierce, scaly, fire-breathing dragons were partners with the devil. The dragons never got the chance to defend themselves.

Ancient Roman soldiers decorated their shields and helmets with dragons. The dragons were symbols of the soldiers' fierceness.

The Aztecs and Mayans, native peoples of North and Central America, believed in dragons. One of the most powerful dragons was the Aztec god Quetzalcoatl. He looked like a large feathered snake.

After Christianity spread through Europe, dragons were seen as evil. This "horned dragon of Hell" appeared in a French book in the late 1800s.

After that, it wasn't possible to be a good dragon in Europe. By medieval times (A.D. 500 to 1500), it was barely possible to be a dragon in Europe at all. That's because saints, knights, and other heroes were always trying to kill dragons.

Why kill a dragon? There were many reasons. For one thing, people in medieval Europe thought that if you ate a dragon's heart, you would

be able to understand the language of animals. If you ate a dragon's tongue, you would never lose an argument. And rubbing your skin with dragon's blood would toughen it enough to turn aside a knife blade.

That kind of fighting edge appealed to the Vikings. These warriors lived in northern Europe during medieval times. Vikings liked to do battle every chance they got. But even with their wartime success, their lives were gloomy. They lived through long winters of bone-rattling cold. Their myths, while powerful, were not designed to warm their hearts. In such a setting, dragons fit right in. The Vikings placed carvings of dragons on the fronts of their ships. The dragons were meant to

A carved dragon's head decorated many Viking ships.

scare enemies. But even Vikings themselves had to worry about dragons. According to Viking lore, dragons would eat Vikings or burn them to a crisp as quickly as anyone else.

Most dragons have kept this hard edge right into the present day. In books and stories, a few dragons have improved their reputations. This is no easy task, though. Even in modern times, people view dragons with fear and suspicion. If dragons want to change their ways (and it's not clear that many of them do), they still have a long way to go.

The famous vampire Dracula, although not a dragon, got his name from the Latin word *draco*, which means "serpent" or "dragon."

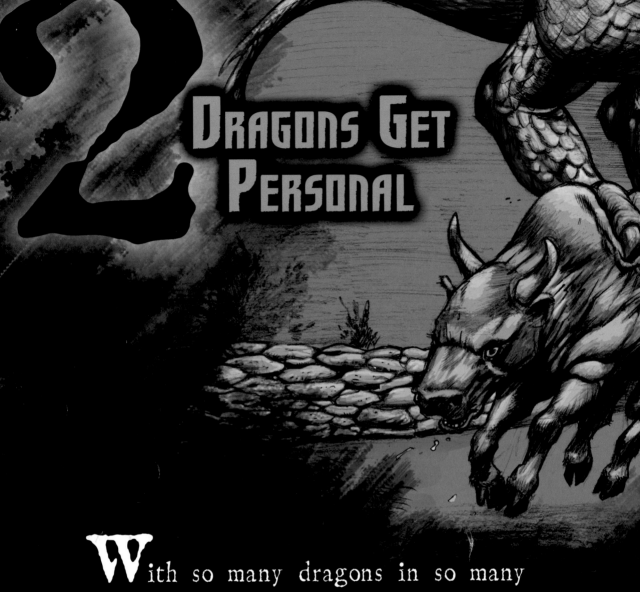

2 Dragons Get Personal

With so many dragons in so many places, it's not surprising that they come in many shapes and sizes. Some dragons have wings. Some don't. Some can talk. Others keep their thoughts to

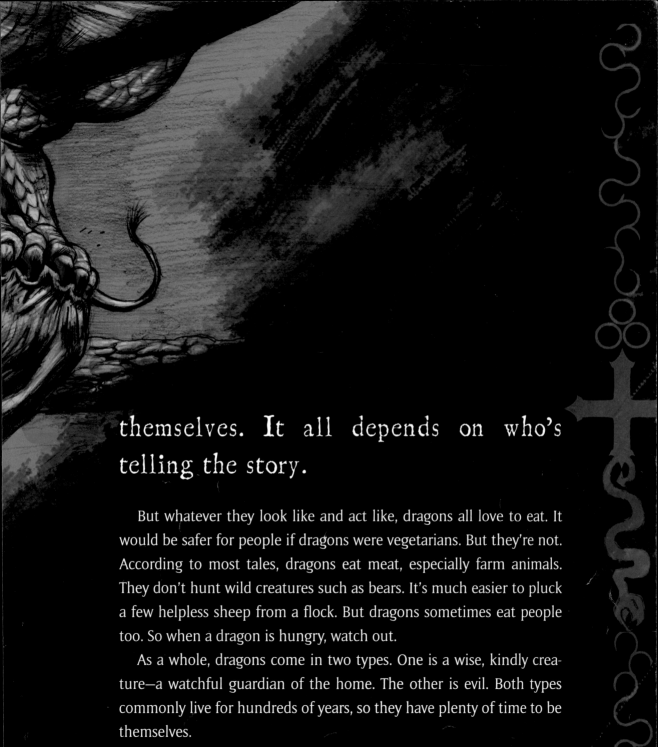

themselves. **It** all depends on who's telling the story.

But whatever they look like and act like, dragons all love to eat. It would be safer for people if dragons were vegetarians. But they're not. According to most tales, dragons eat meat, especially farm animals. They don't hunt wild creatures such as bears. It's much easier to pluck a few helpless sheep from a flock. But dragons sometimes eat people too. So when a dragon is hungry, watch out.

As a whole, dragons come in two types. One is a wise, kindly creature—a watchful guardian of the home. The other is evil. Both types commonly live for hundreds of years, so they have plenty of time to be themselves.

IMAGE IS EVERYTHING

In ancient times, people in Europe thought of dragons as big snakes. They didn't have wings or legs. But during medieval times, artists improved on the dragon image. The classic European dragon, famous in pictures and folktales, looks sort of like an overweight crocodile. It has a large body, strong legs, a winding tail, a pointed ridge along its spine, big wings, sharp teeth, scales, and a head like a lizard's (which may or may not be topped by short horns). Broad nostrils, handy for breathing fire, complete the picture.

Dragons are most often pictured as red, green, or black. But they come in other colors too. The statue above appears on a bridge in Slovenia in Central Europe.

This picture shifts a bit for Asian dragons. They are slimmer than European dragons and usually have no wings. (But they can still fly—which is handy whether you have wings or not.) Some Asian dragons have whiskers on their cheeks and chins. The whiskers make the dragons look either wise or scruffy, depending on your point of view. You might think that having hair near their

This Malaysian carved dragon displays the white whiskers commonly found on Asian dragons.

mouths would make it hard to breathe fire. But Asian dragons don't breathe fire. They can grow their whiskers without worrying about burning them off.

One interesting fact about Asian dragons is that they don't all have the same number of claws on their feet. Chinese and Korean dragons have five claws per foot. Indonesian dragons have four claws, and Japanese dragons have three. The ancient Chinese explained this difference by saying that dragons lost claws as they ventured farther from their Chinese homeland. Not surprisingly, the Japanese had an opposite explanation. In their view, ideal dragons had three claws but gained extra ones as they moved farther and farther from Japan.

In tales from Bulgaria,
in eastern Europe, dragons often fight one
another. Bulgarian dragons also have three heads apiece.
So the heads must really start flying when the fighters go at it.
In other eastern European countries, dragons can have as many
as seven heads. But such dragons don't fight one another. This
makes sense, since all those heads would make a
fight pretty confusing..

Both Europeans and Asians spoke of smaller creatures that looked like dragons but were less famous. Wyverns, for example, were two-legged creatures with sharp claws and snakelike heads. They were also known as lindworms (among other names). Marco Polo, an Italian traveler, reported seeing a wyvern in central Asia in the 1200s. Some wyverns were thought to be good. People put their pictures on flags and shields. But other wyverns were symbols of war and unhappiness.

REAL-LIFE DRAGONS

Even if no one has actually seen a fire-breathing dragon, a few real dragons are wandering around the landscape. For whatever reason, they all live in Southeast Asia and on islands in the Pacific Ocean. These "dragons" are really lizards. Most likely, these real-life dragons inspired many Asian dragon stories.

One example is the frilled dragon. This lizard can grow up to twenty-four inches long from nose to tail. Its color ranges from olive green to brown to almost black. Its name comes from frilly flaps of skin around its neck. The frills sometimes have orange and yellow streaks. They grow bigger when the dragon is angry or frightened. Frilled dragons eat plants, insects, and small animals such as mice.

Somewhat larger (up to three feet—although most of that is tail) is the Chinese water dragon. As you would expect from its name, this greenish brown lizard is at home in the water. It also likes to climb trees, especially to sit on sunny branches. Sometimes pet stores sell Chinese water dragons as pets.

What about a real but scary dragon? There is one—the Komodo dragon. Komodo dragons live on a few Indonesian islands, including one called Komodo. They don't fly or breathe fire. But that doesn't mean they make good pets. Like dragons of legend, they have scaly bodies, sharp claws, and strong teeth.

Two lizards with a dragon name are the frilled dragon *(left)* and the Chinese water dragon *(right)*.

SEARCH FOR A REAL-LIFE DRAGON

People in Asia have known about Komodo dragons *(above)* for thousands of years. But before the 1900s, people in Europe and the United States had never seen Komodo dragons. In 1912 a wealthy adventurer named W. Douglas Burden wanted to learn the truth about Komodo dragons. He led an expedition to the Indonesian island of Komodo. Burden returned to the United States with two living dragons and twelve dead dragons. He gave the living dragons to the Bronx Zoo in New York.

Komodo dragons can grow to be ten feet long and can weigh more than 350 pounds. They need a lot of food. Adult Komodo dragons like to eat deer and wild pigs, but they also snack on birds, snakes, fish, and even younger Komodo dragons.

These creatures don't move too fast. Their hunting strategy is to wait for an animal to get close. Then they make their move. Even if the dragon's prey escapes after a nip, the animal may still be doomed. That's because the Komodo dragon's bite is poisonous.

Komodo dragons have no objections to attacking people. They have done so on at least a few unfortunate (for the people) occasions. But as fearsome as Komodo dragons are, they are no substitute for the dragons of lore.

WHERE'S THE EVIDENCE?

For thousands of years, people believed that dragons were real. But the centuries passed, and no actual dragons turned up. It became harder, at least from a scientific standpoint, to believe in them. By the 1700s, scientists had finally given up the idea that flying, fire-breathing dragons lived among us. Most dragon stories, people came to believe, were probably based on real-life animals such as lizards, crocodiles, alligators, and snakes.

Dragons in Folklore

Dragons, whether from East or West, were always important creatures. Nothing was ordinary about them. From the earliest times, they played important roles in myths and legends around

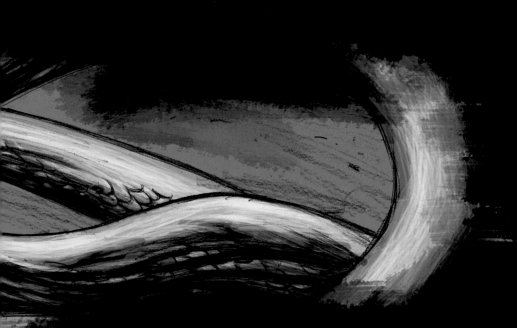

THE STORIES BEGIN

The Middle East is home to some of the oldest dragon tales. For example, according to Sumerian legend, the dragon Zu angered the gods by stealing the Tablets of Law. The sun god, Ninurta, killed Zu for his crime. Dragons were off to a less-than-promising start.

In ancient Egypt, the most feared dragon was Apep. He was angry with Ra, the sun god. Every night as Ra passed through the underworld, Apep tried to swallow him. Most of the time, Ra escaped Apep's jaws. But every so often, Apep swallowed Ra. Then the sun would disappear. Luckily, Ra managed to escape from Apep's belly, so the sun came out again. The Egyptians used this story to explain a solar eclipse—a period when the moon passes between the sun and the earth, briefly blotting out the sun's light.

Another scary Egyptian dragon was Ammut. If you were bad, Ammut would eat your soul. A more helpful Egyptian dragon was Nehebkau. He had the important job of guarding the pharaoh—the Egyptian king—after death.

Dragons also had a place in ancient Greek myths. According to one story, the hero Cadmus killed a dragon. Then an army of men sprang from the dragon's teeth. These soldiers fought one another until only five were left. Those five helped Cadmus found the ancient Greek city of Thebes.

Perhaps the most fearsome dragon of ancient times was the Hydra of Lerna. The legendary Greek hero Hercules fought the Hydra as one of his punishments for committing

This illustration shows Hercules fighting the Hydra. Hercules cuts off the Hydra's heads while his friend Iolaus burns the necks to prevent regrowth.

murder. The Hydra had many heads. Every time Hercules cut one off, a new one grew back. (Hercules eventually solved this problem by burning the Hydra's necks before new heads could appear.)

Constellations are groups of stars in the sky. The Greeks, Romans, and other ancient peoples named constellations for characters in their myths. One constellation is named Draco the Dragon. Its shape looks like a dragon with a long, winding tale.

EASTERN TALES

Farther east, China, Japan, and other Asian nations had many kinds of dragons. Some guarded the homes of gods in the sky. Others kept watch over treasures on earth. Some dragons brought rain to help crops grow.

But not all eastern dragons were nice. In one Japanese tale, an evil dragon eats seven beautiful sisters. The eighth sister, Kushinada, worries that she's next to be eaten. Why? Well, this dragon has eight tails and eight legs, with eight claws on each leg. The dragon seems to like the number eight. This is bad news for Kushinada, the eighth sister. This dragon is big, with eyes that shoot fire. Defeating the dragon in battle does not seem very likely. Just as

According to Chinese legend, a peasant born with a dragon-shaped birthmark might grow up to overthrow the emperor.

the situation is looking bleak, the storm god, Susanoo, arrives on the scene. He makes an offer to Kushinada's parents: he will rescue their daughter if she will become his wife. The parents agree to the marriage. When the dragon arrives, Susanoo offers him a drink of strong liquor. The dragon soon gets drunk—at which point Susanoo kills him.

According to Chinese myth, dragons spent one thousand years in the sea, one thousand years in the mountains, and one thousands years among humans before achieving their full power.

DRAGONS UP NORTH

Up north in Scandinavia, some dragons lived in the land of the gods. The dragon Jörmungandr, for instance, was said to encircle the entire world of Midgard (where people live). To complete the circle, he bit his own tail. Jörmungandr had several run-ins with Thor, the god of thunder and lightning. In their final battle, Thor killed Jörmungandr, but not before the dragon exhaled his poisonous breath into the air. This breath killed Thor a short time later.

Another Scandinavian tale tells of Fafnir, a dragon who started out life as a giant. As a boy, he killed his father so he could take his father's treasures. Then, to guard his riches, he used magic to turn himself into a dragon. After a while, he began to hurt the people who lived nearby. Finally, the hero Siegfried decided to stop Fafnir. Siegfried didn't challenge Fafnir directly. Instead, he dug a trench under the path Fafnir used whenever he went to get a drink. Siegfried waited in the trench.

When Fafnir passed over the trench, Siegfried thrust upward with his sword, wounding the dragon. Then Siegfried jumped out to finish him off.

In this nineteenth century painting by K. Dielitz, Siegfried, a hero of Scandinavian folklore, slays the dragon Fafnir.

BRITISH DRAGONS

In *Beowulf*, the first important written story in English literature, the mighty warrior Beowulf battles a fearsome dragon. Beowulf is no pushover. He has already defeated a monster named Grendel. But he was younger then. And the dragon is no pushover, either. In fact, the dragon is quite angry, thinking someone has stolen its treasure. In the end, Beowulf defeats the dragon, but the victory costs him his own life.

Beowulf was an old man when he fought the dragon. Defeating the dragon sapped the last of his strength, and he died in the dragon's lair.

In Polish legend, a hero named Krak
thought up a trick to defeat a dragon. He hid a chemical
called saltpeter inside the body of a dead sheep. When the
dragon ate the sheep, the saltpeter made him very thirsty. He
couldn't stop drinking water. He drank more and
more water until he finally burst
into thousands of tiny pieces.

In one Welsh myth, Vortigern, the king of all Britain, tries to build a castle. But every time the castle walls go up, a great rumbling from the earth sends them tumbling down again. The king wants an explanation. No one can supply one until a boy comes forward. The rumblings, the boy tells the king, are caused by two dragons fighting deep under the earth. One dragon is red, and the other is white. The boy explains that the white dragon represents people called the Saxons. The red dragon stands for the Welsh people. The king and his advisers don't believe the story at first. But when they dig up the earth under the castle walls, they find the two dragons. And who was this boy? His name was Merlin. When he grew up, he became a great wizard. He served the legendary King Arthur and his knights of the Round Table.

Perhaps the most famous dragon fighter was a knight named George. According to legend, a dragon was threatening a city in North Africa. To keep the dragon satisfied, the townspeople fed it two sheep

each day. But sheep were not always available. At such times, a human sacrifice was needed. In other words, a person had to be fed to the dragon. (You would think the townspeople would make sure to have enough sheep on hand. Apparently, they didn't.) The person was chosen at random. One day the king's daughter had the misfortune of being picked. Luckily for her, George arrived before the dragon did. George waited for the dragon and defeated it in battle. For killing the dragon and other good deeds, George became a saint in the Christian Church.

Saint George slays the dragon in this 1586 woodcut from England.

4 Dragons Take Flight

Modern people still tell stories about dragons. The old myths and legends live on. Around the beginning of the 1900s, authors began including dragons in brand-new stories. Some writers spun their stories around the old dragon

tales. Other writers took dragons in new directions. Eventually, cartoonists and filmmakers got into the act.

DRAGONS IN PRINT

One of the first children's books to focus on dragons was *The Reluctant Dragon* (1898) by the British writer Kenneth Grahame. In this takeoff on the tale of Saint George, a shepherd discovers a dragon sleeping in a cave. The shepherd and most of the other villagers want George to kill the dragon. But the shepherd's son, having read a lot of fairy tales, knows that not every dragon is fierce. When George arrives, the boy convinces him to meet the dragon. After that, the characters come up with a much happier ending (especially for the dragon).

In modern China, groups of people wearing large dragon costumes take part in New Year's Day parades.

Some of the most powerful dragons in fiction live in Middle Earth—a world created by another British author, J. R. R. Tolkien. The best known of these dragons comes from Tolkien's *The Hobbit* (1937). This is the story of Bilbo Baggins, a somewhat timid creature called a hobbit. Some dwarves mistake Bilbo for a master thief. They ask him to help defeat a dragon named Smaug. Smaug is cruel and greedy. He has captured all the dwarves' treasure. Bilbo does not actually kill Smaug. But he does help bring about Smaug's downfall.

J. R. R. Tolkien, creator of the dragon Smaug, relaxes against a tree in Oxford, England, shortly before his death in 1973.

Just as powerful as J. R. R. Tolkien's Smaug—but more majestic—are the dragons in Ursula Le Guin's stories of Earthsea. Books in the Earthsea series include *A Wizard of Earthsea* and *The Farthest Shore*, which focus on the adventures of the wizard Sparrowhawk.

My Father's Dragon (1948), a book by Ruth Gannett, takes a more lighthearted approach to dragons. The book tells of a boy named Elmer Elevator. He sets out to rescue a baby dragon in a distant place called Wild Island. Does Elmer have a sword or other weapons to help him? No—but he does have pink lollipops, chewing gum, rubber bands, and a comb. It turns out that with these tools, a true hero can always succeed.

Back in the almost real word is 1991's *Jeremy Thatcher, Dragon Hatcher.* In this book by Bruce Coville, twelve-year-old Jeremy Thatcher has problems enough for a boy his age. His teachers are giving him a hard time, and there's a girl—Mary Lou Hutton—whom he wants to avoid.

"Puff the Magic Dragon" is a well-known song. The folk group Peter, Paul, and Mary recorded the tune in the 1960s. Puff was a dragon that lived by the sea. A little boy named Jackie Paper loved Puff. But when Jackie grew up, he forgot about Puff.

Jeremy buys a strange egg in a small magic shop. The egg hatches, and out comes a dragon—a dragon that only Jeremy and Mary Lou can see. Then Jeremy has a whole new set of problems to worry about.

Anne McCaffrey has woven dragons into science fiction in her Dragonriders of Pern series. The stories take place on the planet Pern. On Pern, dragons (and their riders) regularly save people from Thread, deadly spores that fall from space. If Thread reaches the ground, it does terrible damage. So it must be burned while still in the air. Pern's dragons come in different sizes, strengths, and colors—gold, bronze, brown, blue, and green.

DRAG-ANIMATION

No matter what kind of dragon someone writes about, putting dragons on the page is not that hard. Drawing pictures of dragons is pretty easy too. But showing dragons in the movies is much harder. Between flying and breathing fire, dragons are difficult to show realistically on film.

For many years, dragons in the movies usually took animated form. But a cartoon dragon is not necessarily a cute dragon. For instance, in Walt Disney Pictures' *Sleeping Beauty* (1959), the evil fairy Maleficent turns herself into a fire-breathing dragon to keep her plans from being ruined. It's a scary moment for Prince Phillip, who faces her with only a sword, a shield, and his trusty horse. But all is not lost. Even the mighty Maleficent is no match for the power of true love.

In this scene from Disney's *Sleeping Beauty*, Prince Phillip faces the evil fairy Maleficent in dragon form.

DUNGEONS AND DRAGONS

In 1973 Gary Gygax and Dave Arneson created a game called Dungeons and Dragons. The rules require players to take on roles (and not always human ones) and face other characters in different situations. The game includes fantasy characters, secret maps, and lucky rolls of the dice. Dragons are important, of course. But they share space in the game with giants, elves, goblins, and other creatures. The game has inspiredmany books and a couple of movies.

Players Handbooks (*above*) for Dungeons and Dragons give specific details about the many different characters in the game, including dragons.

Cute is the key word in *Pete's Dragon* (1977). In this film, Pete wants to get away from the mean parents who have adopted him. The movie is live action—except for Pete's best friend, Elliott, an animated dragon. Pete and Elliott escape. They are pursued by the wicked Dr. Terminus. Dr. Terminus is defeated, as villains usually are, and Pete and Elliott get their happy endings.

Another movie dragon appears in *Mulan* (1998), also from Walt Disney Pictures. The first Mulan was the heroine in a Chinese poem written about sixteen hundred years ago. The poem tells of a girl who dresses as a man to

Pete hangs out with his lovable dragon friend, Elliott, in the 1977 film *Pete's Dragon*.

take her father's place in the army. In Disney's version, Mulan has a sidekick, a small red dragon named Mushu. Throughout the adventure, Mushu comments on the action. There's nothing fierce about this dragon. He's along only to provide comedy.

In the animated movie *Shrek* (2001), the ogre Shrek must rescue Princess Fiona from an evil dragon. At least the dragon *seems* evil. After all, it's holding the princess prisoner. But the dragon proves useful in the end when he eats the wicked Lord Farquaad.

Dragon and Donkey share a moment in *Shrek*.

Actor Eddie Murphy played roles in both *Mulan* and *Shrek*. In *Mulan* he played Mushu the dragon. In *Shrek* he played Shrek's sidekick, the donkey. But Murphy never appeared in the films. He only provided voices for the animated characters.

DRAGONS GET REAL

Dragonslayer (1981) was one of the first movies to use special effects to create a live-action dragon. The film tells the tale of a dragon that menaces a kingdom. A wizard and his helper try to save a king's daughter from being the dragon's next meal. The dragon doesn't have many scenes—special effects are expensive, after all—but it looks almost like the real thing (if dragons were real, that is).

Fifteen years later came *Dragonheart* (1996). This story tells of a dragon slayer named Bowen. He is supposed to kill Draco, the last dragon around. Instead, they form a partnership and travel to different villages. Draco pretends to threaten the villagers so that Bowen can "defeat" him. After the fake battle, the villagers pay Bowen for rescuing them from

Draco lights a campfire in this scene from *Dragonheart*.

Draco. The plot grows more complicated when the partners learn that an evil king has a part of Draco's heart inside him.

Reign of Fire (2002) not only makes dragons look real on screen. It also sets them in the present day. This fantasy-science fiction combination starts with the idea that dragons have been awakened at the turn of the twenty-first century. Seemingly unstoppable, the

Dragon Tales came to television in 1999. The show follows the adventures of six-year-old Emmy and her four-year-old brother, Max. They travel to Dragon Land, where they have bilingual (English and Spanish) adventures.

dragons reduce modern civilization to ashes. But the dragons have one weakness. There is only one male dragon. Kill him, and the species will die out. The film's script is not as impressive as its dragons. But the movie is still frightening.

Whether dragons exist or not, no doubt they are brutish beasts. Dragons may inspire your imagination. But don't be in a hurry to go looking for them. Sure, it would be exciting to meet a dragon. Just remember, you might live (for a short time) to regret it.

The popular Harry Potter books and films include dragons. In *Harry Potter and the Goblet of Fire* (2005), Harry has a run-in with a dragon called a Hungarian Horntail.

Selected Bibliography

Briggs, Katharine. *An Encyclopedia of Fairies, Hobgoblins, Brownies, Bogies and Other Supernatural Creatures.* New York: Pantheon Books, 1976.

Gould, Charles. *Dragons, Unicorns and Sea Serpents.* Mineola, NY: Dover Publications, Inc., 2002.

Hague, Michael, ed. *The Book of Dragons.* New York: William Morrow and Company, 1995.

Lehner, Ernst, and Johanna Lehner. *Big Book of Dragons, Monsters and Other Mythical Creatures.* Mineola, NY: Dover Publications, Inc., 2004.

Rose, Carol. *Giants, Monsters and Dragons: An Encyclopedia of Folklore, Legend and Myth.* New York: W. W. Norton and Company, 2000.

Simpson, Jacqueline. *British Dragons.* London: B. T. Batsford Ltd., 1980.

Steer, Donald A. *Dr. Ernest Drake's Dragonology: The Complete Book of Dragons.* Cambridge, MA: Candlewick Press, 2003.

Further Reading and Websites

The Circle of the Dragon

http://www.blackdrago.com/outline.htm

This site examines dragons from different cultures, including those from ancient times.

Coville, Bruce. *Jeremy Thatcher, Dragon Hatcher.* New York: Harcourt Children's Books, 2002. This beautifully illustrated book follows the ups and downs of Jeremy, his classmate Mary Lou Hutton, and a dragon named Tiamat.

Dragonorama

http://www.dragonorama.com/western/norse.html

This site offers tales of dragons from many different cultures, organized by place of origin.

Engdahl, Sylvia Louise. *Enchantress from the Stars*. New York: Atheneum, 1970. In this novel for young readers, a boy must destroy a wicked dragon on a distant planet.

Funke, Cornelia. *Dragon Rider*. Frome, UK: Chicken House, 2004. This novel for young readers tells of a brave dragon named Firedrake. Accompanied by an orphaned boy and a grumpy fairy, Firedrake takes a dangerous journey to the Rim of Heaven.

Gannet, Ruth Stiles. *My Father's Dragon*. New York: Random House Books for Young Readers, 1987. This classic, originally published in 1948, will delight readers with its story of Elmer Elevator and a flying baby dragon.

LeGuin, Ursula K. *A Wizard of Earthsea*. Berkeley, CA: Parnassas Press, 1968. A young wizard must face inner demons as well as other problems (including a dragon) as he strives to reach his full potential.

McCaffrey, Anne. *Dragonsong*. New York: Atheneum, 1977. Musically talented Menolly finds herself caring for nine baby dragons.

Paolini, Christopher. *Eldest*. New York: Knopf Books for Young Readers, 2005. Young Eragon and his dragon, Saphira, must save the land of Alagaesia from the wicked emperor Galbatorix. This title is the second book in Paolini's Inheritance trilogy.

Rowling, J. K. *Harry Potter and the Goblet of Fire*. New York: Scholastic, 2000. In the fourth installment of his adventures, Harry must overcome an assortment of obstacles—including dragons—in his quest for the Goblet of Fire.

Tolkien, J. R. R. *The Hobbit*. Boston: Houghton Mifflin, 1938. A quest to retrieve treasure from a fierce dragon takes a hobbit named Bilbo Baggins on the adventure of a lifetime.

Wrede, Patricia. *The Enchanted Forest Chronicles*. San Diego: Magic Carpet Books, 2003.

Four favorite dragon tales—*Dealing with Dragons, Searching for Dragons, Calling on Dragons*, and *Talking to Dragons*—are offered together in this boxed set. The books follow the adventures of Cimorene, a princess with a mind of her own.

MOVIES

Dragonheart. Universal City, CA: MCA Home Video, 1996.

A dragon slayer teams up with a dragon to make money. But their fate takes a different turn when they must fight an evil king.

Dragonslayer. Los Angeles: Paramount, 2003.

One of the first live-action dragons appears in this 1981 film, re-released in DVD format.

Mulan. Burbank, CA: Walt Disney Home Entertainment, 2004.

This animated version of an old Chinese folktale features a girl named Mulan and a small red dragon.

Reign of Fire. Burbank, CA: Touchstone/Disney, 2002.

Heartthrob Matthew McConaughey stars in this action-packed dragon movie.

Shrek. Glendale, CA: DreamWorks Video, 2001.

This tale features an ogre, a fire-breathing dragon, and plenty of adventure.

Index

About the Author

Stephen Krensky is the author of many fiction and nonfiction books for children, including titles in the On My Own Folklore series and *Frankenstein*, *Werewolves*, *Vampires*, *The Mummy*, and *Bigfoot*. When he isn't hunched over his computer, he makes school visits and teaches writing workshops. In his free time, he enjoys playing tennis and softball and reading books by other people. Krensky lives in Massachusetts with his wife, Joan, and their family.

Photo Acks

The images in this book are used with the permission of: © Fortean Picture Library, pp. 2-3, 9, 19, 32; © North Wind Picture Archives, pp. 8, 13, 14; © Image Select/Art Resource, NY, p. 10; © Scala/Art Resource, NY, p. 11; © Steve Vidler/SuperStock, p. 18; © Tom Brakefield/SuperStock, p. 21 (left); © ZSSD/SuperStock, pp. 21 (right), 22; © Hulton Archive/Getty Images, p. 26; © Bettmann/CORBIS, p. 29; Mary Evans Picture Library, p. 30; © Pierre Andrieu/AFP/Getty Images, p. 34; Library of Congress, p. 35; © The Walt Disney Company. Image courtesy Everett Collection, pp. 37, 39; © Sam Lund/Independent Picture Service, p. 38; © Dreamworks SKG/Courtesy Everett Collection, p. 40; Courtesy of Universal Studios Licensing, LLLP. All Rights Reserved. p. 41; © Sesame Workshop/Columbia Tristar Television/Courtesy Everett Collection, p. 42; Illustrations by Bill Hauser/Independent Picture Service, pp. 6-7, 16-17, 24-25, 33-34; All page backgrounds illustrated by Bill Hauser.

Cover: Bill Hauser/Independent Picture Service.